Let's Talk About Life

Let's Talk About Life

JAMIE BUCKINGHAM

John Buckingham, M.D., M.P.H.
Medical Consultant

Creation House
Strang Communications Company
Altamonte Springs, Florida

Revised Edition 1986
Copyright © 1986 by Strang Communications Company
Altamonte Springs, Florida 32714
All rights reserved
Printed in the United States of America

This book or parts thereof may not be reproduced in any form without permission of the publishers.

Library of Congress Catalog Number #86-61987
ISBN #0-930525-07-8

To our children:
Bruce
Robin
Bonnie
Tim
Sandy
From diapers to maternity clothes
they have forced me to discover the
real meaning of sex: LOVE.

CONTENTS

Foreword 11

Introduction 13

Chapter One
Let's Measure 15

Chapter Two
Where Did You Come From? 23

Chapter Three
The Baby Grows Inside the Mother 43

Chapter Four
The Baby Is Born 53

Chapter Five
Girl or Boy? 61

Chapter Six
Growing Up 71

Chapter Seven
Growing and Learning 83

Chapter Eight
Looking Forward to Changes 95

Words You Should Know 107

Some Other Helpful Books 111

FOREWORD

I grew up in a home where sex was never mentioned.

I remember, when I was about 11 years old, asking my father candid questions about the changes my body was going through. He was too "proper" to tell me and said something like, "One day you'll understand."

I did understand one day—but not until I had gotten into a lot of trouble. How much better it would have been had my parents taught me the "facts of life" in language I could understand. Then I would not have to think sex was something "dirty," "improper," or only for married people to discuss.

We are all sexual beings, from the moment we appear as boys or girls. God's plan calls for us to be educated beings also—not just about our bodies but about His purpose for our bodies.

No subject arouses the emotions as quickly, and leads into danger just as quickly, as the subject of sex. I do not believe it can be taught in a secular, amoral atmosphere. Sex can no more be discussed apart from God than we can discuss the future apart from God. Yet it must be discussed. And no one is more qualified than loving parents who, in the normal course of the day's activities, explain to their children how the body functions, why it functions and the purpose of each organ.

My wife and I have had five children—two boys and three girls. We've had a lot of fun discussing these things with them. I'm grateful my boys have not grown up wondering and my girls have not grown up afraid. They all looked forward to marriage and are now passing along these same concepts to their children.

My brother, John, a medical doctor specializing in family practice, checked this manuscript for medical accuracy and added a few things here and there. The book is for parents to use with their pre-adolescent children. And who knows, maybe parents will learn a thing or two as well.

Jamie Buckingham
Palm Bay, Florida

INTRODUCTION

In a society where children are constantly bombarded with raw sex from the mass media, youngsters are asking questions earlier and earlier. Believing that the Bible holds the answers and that the place for sex education is in the home, Creation House offers this book to offset the damaging half-truths and twisted concepts coming from recent authors—and to supplement the basically amoral sex education children are now receiving in the public classroom. Designed to be used in the home, the church, in neighborhood home study classes, or in Christian schools, it approaches the subject of sex, reproduction, human anatomy, and physical and spiritual growth with reverence, sacredness and beauty.

Creation House
Altamonte Springs, FL 32714
Printed in U.S.A.

CHAPTER ONE
Let's Measure

Let's Measure

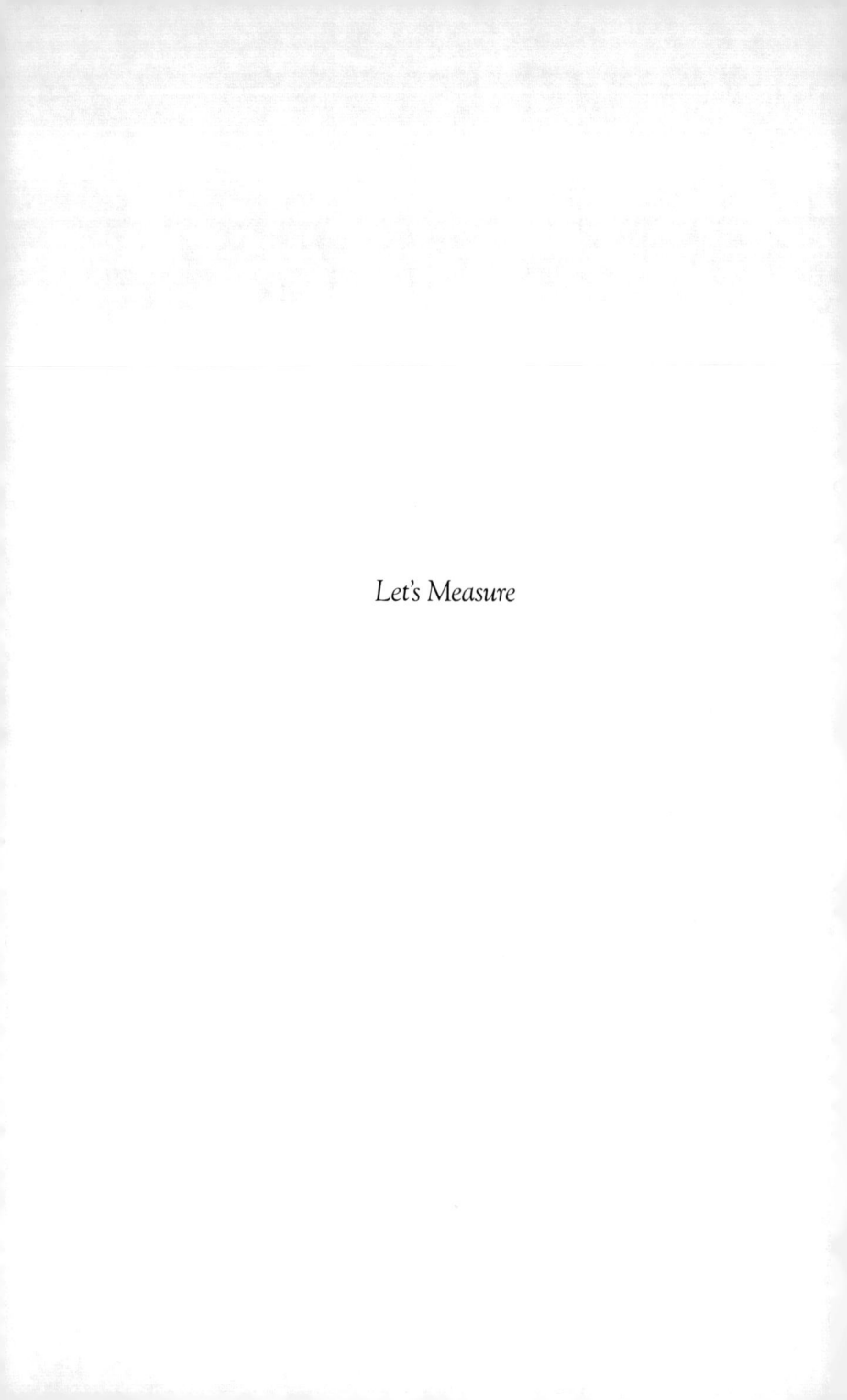

When we were children we lived in a big two-story house in Florida. Every New Year's Day my daddy would call the five children (four boys and a baby sister), and we'd march up the stairs to the big bathroom where he'd open the closet door and get out the yardstick. One by one we'd stand up against the door, our backs as stiff as could be and our necks stretched out as far as we could stretch them. Daddy would lay the yardstick flat on our heads and make a mark on the door.

As the years went by, it became a game to see who would grow the most in a single year. Many times after we'd gotten out of the bathtub, we'd hop across the floor and get Mother or Daddy to measure us—just to see how fast we were growing.

Sometimes now I go back to the big old house and go upstairs and open the closet door and look at those marks. Funny thing—when my oldest brother stopped growing he was 5'9'' tall and weighed 165 pounds. But the youngest brother didn't stop growing until he was 6'2'' tall and weighed 200 pounds. And our baby sister grew to almost as tall as the older brother. Each one of us was different, but all of us were well and strong. And God loved us all regardless of what size we were.

Growing tall and gaining weight are not the only ways of growing that you will be reading about in this book. Growth—getting taller and gaining weight—is a wonderful, mysterious process that no one knows very much about. Even doctors don't know all the secrets about why boys and girls reach different heights when they are grown. Only God knows. Clever men can make things—like helicopters, computers and even rockets to go to the moon. But no one can make a boy or girl like you. The Bible says: "Know ye that the Lord he is God; it is he that hath made us, and not we ourselves..." (Psalm 100:3). And growing up is part of what God intends for each of us.

When the boy Jesus was 12 years old He began to shoot up like a weed. Not only did He grow physically, but He grew "in wisdom and stature and in favour with God and man" (Luke 2:52). This means that He was becoming more and more useful and well-loved by all who knew Him. This is God's purpose for your life also.

Growing up is a curious thing. Babies are about 20 inches long when they are born. In the first year they are born, they will usually grow another 10 inches. In their second year they will grow about half that much, so that usually by the time a child reaches his 2nd birthday he will be almost as tall as a yardstick. After that, children grow more slowly. No one knows exactly why God does it this way—we just know He does.

Let's Measure

Think what it would be like if we grew as much every year as we grow our first year. Why, by the time we were in the sixth grade we'd be almost 11 feet tall! And your baby sister, who is only 3 would be over four feet tall—but she still wouldn't know how to talk, think or act like a grown person. Fortunately your growth slows down, and you have time to start learning how to think and act like grown-ups while you are reaching adult size.

When you reach the age of 10 or 12, you suddenly start to grow rapidly again—but not as fast as when you were a baby. Some children start growing rapidly before this time and some wait until they are almost 16. This growing spurt may last for three or four years, and by the time you've finished you'll be as tall as you'll ever be as an adult. Perhaps you have some classmates or friends who have already begun to spurt ahead.

Boys in the sixth and seventh grades are often surprised when some of the girls in their class at school seem to grow taller suddenly and leave the boys behind. In a couple of years the boys will begin to catch up, and in the end, most boys are taller than most girls.

By the time you're 18 or 19 you will have stopped growing taller.

So, as you can see, there are four stages in the way you grow taller. Fast (as a baby); slow (after you start to school); fast (in junior high); slow (in senior high); then stop.

But there was a time in your life when you grew faster than any of these times mentioned. Do you know when it was? It was during the nine months before you were born. This was the beginning of the first stage of growth. You were living inside your mother's body. When your life first began you were so small you could have been

LET'S TALK ABOUT LIFE

seen only with a strong magnifying glass. Soon you grew to be the size of a grain of rice. Then in a few more days, you were the size of a green pea. In just a matter of a few more days you had grown to be as big as a walnut. You kept growing until you were as big as a cantaloupe, and when you were born, you probably weighed about six or seven pounds. If you ask your mother, she can probably tell you exactly how much you weighed and how long you were when you were born. How big were you?

But where did you come from in the *very beginning*? How did you first begin? When did you really become alive? How did you get out from inside your mother? Why are you growing in the way you are now? All these things will be explained in this booklet, along with a lot of other answers to mysterious questions about which you probably have already been wondering. Why do some babies turn out to be boys—and some girls? Why are some people tall, others short? Is there any way of telling how big you'll be when you grow up? And, oh yes! Why do you eventually stop growing? Why don't you just keep growing and growing until you're a giant? This story of how you and other boys and girls started life and how you grow will help to answer these and many other questions.

But the important thing to remember is that it is God who makes life—and it is God who has told us how to live in order to please Him.

Let's Measure

FILL IN BLANKS:

1. I was born on (date)_____.
2. At birth I weighed ____ pounds and was ____ inches long.
3. I now weigh ____ pounds and am ____ inches tall.
4. Can you make yourself grow taller?

    Yes ____ No ____
5. When I was born my hair was blonde ____, brunette ____, red ____, bald ____.
6. My hair is now colored _____.

CHAPTER TWO

Where Did You Come From?

Where Did You Come From?

All life comes from God

Life is in cells

Life in the mother comes from egg cells

Life in the father comes from sperm cells

A story of love—how the sperm cell finds the egg cell

The two most important people in your life are your mother and father, because without them you wouldn't be here today. Perhaps you've noticed, as you study the lives of famous people, that they always talk about their mothers and fathers. The Bible has a great deal to say about Jesus' mother. In Bible times the people were often called by their parents' names. Simon Peter was known as Simon Bar-Jonah. The word "bar" means "son of," so Simon's name was actually Simon, son of Jonah. His father's name, you see, was Jonah. Thus we can see how important our mothers and fathers really are.

If we're going to talk about where you came from and how you grow, we need to talk about your parents. When you talk with them, I imagine their story is something like this:

Your mother and daddy have not always lived

together. One time, a long time ago, your daddy was just a little boy and your mother a little girl. They grew up and met each other and decided they loved each other so much they wanted to live together—always. So they were married. Have they ever told you about their wedding? Maybe you've seen some pictures they had made of their wedding. It may have been in a church, or just a small wedding in a home. But wherever it was, there was something special about it because your father and mother were in love and they made a promise to God that they would live with and love each other the rest of their lives. It was a happy day for them. Your mother looked very beautiful and your daddy was very proud.

After they were married they found a place to live and helped each other make a home. Home is where you want to go when you are tired, hungry, or afraid. It is where you feel comfortable.

Have you ever seen birds making a nest? The father bird flies off and picks up twigs and little sticks and brings them back to the bush or tree where the mother bird weaves them all together and makes a nest where she can lay her eggs. Your father worked to earn money to buy what was needed (maybe your mother had to work too), and your mother made the house comfortable and home-like. Your father and mother helped make the home by doing the things each knew how to do. After a while, because your father and mother loved each other, and because God has told men and women who live together that they ought to have children, the time came when you were born. So you see, you were born because your mother and father loved each other very much, because they wanted to have a little baby they could share their love with, and because it is God's plan that men and women should have babies, and take care of them, and raise them to love the Lord also.

Sometimes children do not know who their real parents are. Perhaps their real parents are dead—or no longer live with their children. Now the children live with someone other than their real parents. Even so, it is your real father and mother who gave you life and even if you do not know them, God does. He blessed them by giving you to them—even if it was only for a short time. Remember this: God loves all babies and instructs parents (if they will listen) how to love and care for their children.

But where did you come from? Well, let's see if we can find an answer to that question.

All Life Comes From God

God is the Creator of all life. The Bible tells us that in the beginning of the world God made everything—four legged animals, birds, trees, fish, flowers, people. What would have happened if He had forgotten to plan a way for these living creatures to keep coming into the world? Suppose He had just made the very first birds, the first fish, the first cats, and the first elephants but failed to give them a way and a desire to make more animals like themselves. It wouldn't have taken long before all the living things on this earth died, and it would have been a lifeless, barren planet like the moon—with no life as we know it.

But God is very wise, and He could look into the future and see that He would also have to create some way that the living things on the earth could reproduce, that is, give birth to little ones like themselves.

The Bible tells us that there were only two people in the beginning—Adam and Eve. Now just think of all the people there are in the world today. How did they all get here? Where did they all come from? The Bible says that when the great flood came, many years later, that Noah took only two of each kind of living animal into the ark—one male and one female. All the other animals (except the fish) drowned. But look at all the animals we have around us now—dogs, cats, horses, cows—not to mention all the birds and wild animals. And if you go out in your yard some day and look around the grass, you will see hundreds, maybe even thousands, of tiny little animals that live close to the earth: ants, bugs, spiders, and many other tiny creatures, all made by God.

Where did they all come from? They each came from others just like themselves. The two cows that Noah took on the ark had baby calves, and soon there were many new cows on the new earth. These cows "mated" with each other (as did all the other animals), and it didn't take too long before there were more than anyone could count. No wonder God says in the Bible, "Every beast of the forest is mine, and the cattle upon a thousand hills" (Psalm 50:10).

This is what happened with people, too. God created the first human life. He made Adam out of the dust of the earth, and then He made Eve, Adam's wife. But God made human beings different from all the other creatures. They were a separate creation and were made with a spiritual nature—not just a physical nature. Even though people are similar to animals, they are very different also—because human beings are made in the "image of God," and God "breathed into them the breath of life." This is a spiritual quality not found in animals, and it is one of the important things that makes us dif-

Where Did You Come From?

ferent from all the rest of God's creatures.

God told Adam and Eve that they should have babies. Then their children had children and so on until today we have people living almost everywhere. You see, we all come from someone just before us, and so all people in the world are somewhat related to each other.

The Bible teaches us that when God made everything in the beginning He made at least two of each kind. He called one *male* and the other *female*. The male is the father and the female is the mother.

God loves both the mother and the father and wants them to share in the joy of having a baby. If having a baby were only the mother's job—then the baby would belong to her. If God had let just the father have a baby, then the baby would have belonged just to him. But God wanted the mother and father to share in having a baby, so the baby would belong to both. Therefore, both father and mother loved the child.

We think this is a wonderful way—don't you? This plan allows the mother and father to love the baby equally. It also makes the mother and father love each other more than ever because when the baby comes, they know that each one had a part in making their new little baby.

It's a strange thing, but with so many smart people in the world, no one has yet figured out how to create human life without having both a mother and a father. Why? Because God created the first life and said it was to be passed on by mothers and fathers, and since life comes only from God, man has not been able to create it himself.

Whenever a new life comes into the world, it must start from a similar being that already has life. Your

LET'S TALK ABOUT LIFE

life started from the life that your mother and father gave to you. Their life came from their mothers and fathers (your grandparents) and so on all the way back to Adam and Eve—and it was God who gave to each of them this life also. "And the Lord God formed man of the dust of the ground, and breathed into his nostrils the breath of life; and man became a living soul" (Genesis 2:7). "So God created man in his own image, in the image of God created he him; male and female created he them. And God blessed them, and God said unto them, Be fruitful, and multiply, and replenish the earth..." (Genesis 1:27-28).

Life Is in Cells

If you have a chance to look at a live leaf under a microscope, you will see that it is made up of many small parts called cells. All cells have a thin wall that surrounds a fluid material that is remarkable because it is living. Many living things—some animals and some plants—are made of only one cell. Others are made of two cells, or a hundred cells, or billions of cells. When these cells live together in perfect harmony, they make up a living object—such as a rabbit, a tree, a boy or a girl.

In a human being there are many different kinds of cells. There are muscle cells, skin cells, bone cells, nerve cells, blood cells and many other kinds. And there are two very special kinds of cells that are needed to start the life of a new human being. Your mother has one kind of cell in her body, called an *egg cell*. Your father has another kind in his body called a *sperm cell*. It takes one of each kind of cell, united into one, to begin a new life. It is necessary to have both a father and a mother. One without the other is not enough, and could

Where Did You Come From?

not make a new life.

Life in the Mother Comes From Egg Cells

When we say egg cells, you probably think of a chicken egg, the kind your mother might fix for breakfast. Now try to imagine, if you can, a chicken egg so small that it would take more than 200 of them placed in a row to reach one inch. If the light is just right, and your eyes are very sharp, you might just barely see one without a magnifying glass, if they were out in the open. But these tiny egg cells are inside your mother's body where they cannot be seen. Each is round, like a tiny ball; it has a very thin covering around it, and inside the wall there is material for a new life.

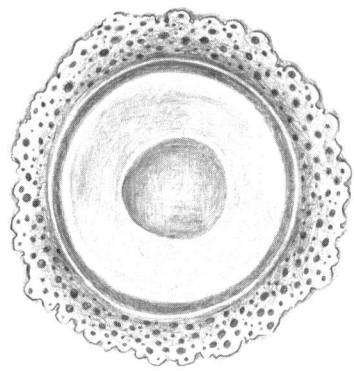

This material inside the egg is alive—but it cannot grow by itself. It lives only a short time, and then it dies, unless it meets a cell from your daddy's body, called a sperm. It is at this time that it will begin a new life. (But we'll discuss that later.)

The egg cell comes from a special gland inside your

mother called an *ovary* (OH-vuh-ree). Girls have two ovaries, each about the size of a medium marshmallow. They are in the lower part of the *abdomen* (AB-duh-men). Doctors, nurses and other people often speak of the abdomen as the belly. (You might have called it your stomach.)

When a baby girl is born, the ovaries are already in her body, with small egg cells in each ovary. Most girls are about 12 or 13 years old when the ovaries begin to change (remember, they are, even then, very small), and the partly grown egg cells become full-grown egg cells. After that, about once a month, one fully grown egg cell leaves one or the other ovary and is then ready to unite with a sperm cell from a father. If there are no sperm cells, then, in a few days, the cell leaves the body. Another egg cell is already getting ready to leave the ovary the next month. This monthly cycle of an egg leaving the ovary continues until a woman is about 45 or so years old. From then on, no more egg cells leave the ovaries.

Each egg leaves the ovary by passing through a small tube called the *fallopian* (fal-O-pee-un) tube. There is a tube for each ovary. The egg cell travels through the tube to another part of the body called the *uterus* (YOO-ter-us), or *womb* (woom). The uterus is in the lowest part of the abdomen and is the place where the new life will grow until it is time for the baby to be born. The uterus is about the size and shape of a pear and lies "upside down" in the mother. The hollow fallopian tubes enter the large part on each side.

A smooth passage called the *vagina* (va-JY-nuh) connects the uterus with the outside of the body. The outside opening of the vagina is between a girl's legs, where

Where Did You Come From?

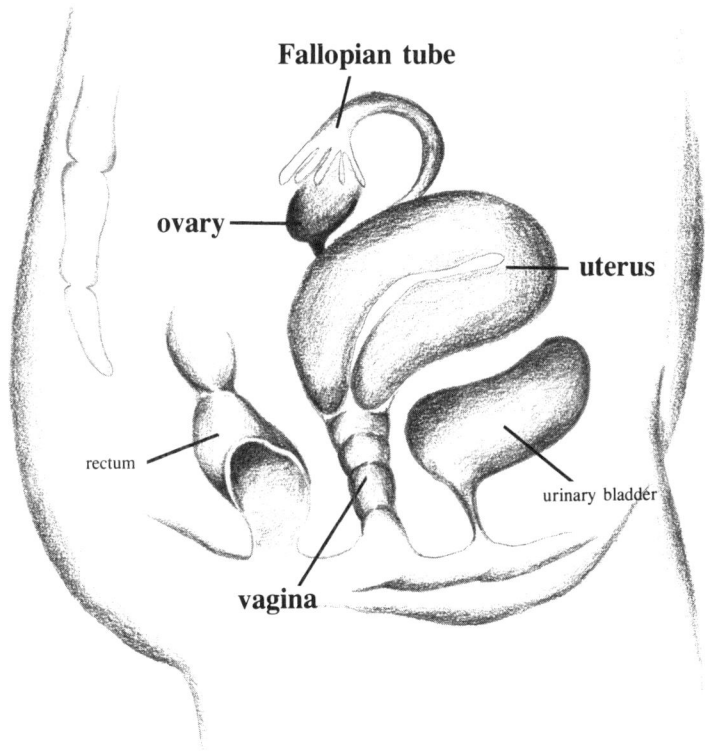

it is protected by soft folds of skin and flesh. Directly in front of the vaginal opening is another small opening where the liquid waste from the body (urine) is expelled. Another opening, for bowel movements, is some distance in back of it. All are quite separate, and young girls frequently don't realize there is "another" opening. Boys and girls should be careful not to put anything into any of the body's openings for they may hurt themselves or cause an infection and be sick. If this should happen, you should tell your parents and a doctor so they can help you get well.

Perhaps now you can see how wonderfully God has planned the body of girls and women. You can also see how, from the time a girl becomes old enough to start thinking of marriage, God has already prepared her body so she can have a baby.

Girls have ovaries, a uterus, and a vagina. Boys do not have these parts of the body.

Most of the eggs that leave the ovaries travel through one of the tubes, through the uterus, into the vagina and out of the body. But not all of them!

Life in the Father Comes From Sperm Cells

Sometimes an egg cell stays in the mother's uterus and starts growing into a baby. What causes this? This happens when a sperm cell from the father joins the egg cell made by the mother.

When a sperm cell comes in contact with an egg cell, the egg and the sperm merge together to make one new cell. The new cell is then called a *fertilized* (FER-ti-lized) *egg cell*, and it usually grows into a baby. Remember, a mother cannot start a baby by herself; she must have the sperm cell from the father. When the two cells meet—the mother's egg and the father's sperm—then a *new life* comes into being. This is how you got started, how I got started, and how every living person came into being.

In the Bible, God told Adam and Eve that they should be "one flesh." Yet they were two people. How can two people become one flesh? Perhaps now you can see

Where Did You Come From?

the answer. Two people can become one flesh when the egg cell of the mother receives the sperm cell of the father, and instead of there being two separate cells, there is now a completely new cell—and out of this new cell grows a whole new life: a baby.

In the book of Ephesians, the apostle Paul speaks of the same process when he says, "For this cause shall a man leave his father and mother, and shall be joined unto his wife, and they two shall be one flesh! This is a great mystery..." (Ephesians 5:31-32). Paul is right; it is a great mystery. In fact it is one of the greatest and most wonderful mysteries of life—how two cells, both

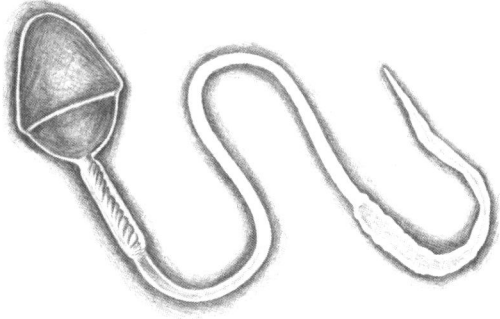

of which contain a part of life given from God, can meet together inside the female and out of this meeting grows a wholly new human being.

Sperm cells grow in two parts of the father's body called *testicles* (TESS-ti-kals). The testicles are in a small sac of skin resembling a round, deflated rubber balloon called the *scrotum* (SKROH-tum) that hangs gently from the lower abdomen just in front and between the legs of boys. They are on the outside of the body.

The sperm cells are much smaller than the egg cells,

and the fully grown testicles make millions of them. They are shaped something like a microscopic tadpole, bigger at one end with a long slender tail. They live in a liquid, much as tadpoles live in water, and they can move very rapidly by swishing their tails. When the sperm cells leave the testicles, they go through a series of small tubes that connect to the *penis* (PEE-nis). The penis is just in front of the testicles, and is shaped something like a finger, but without bones and quite soft. There is a small opening in the end of the penis that the boy also uses to urinate. It is through this opening that the sperm cells leave the body too. However, sperm cells and urine cannot come out of the penis at the same time.

When a baby boy is born he already has testicles and a penis. As he grows, the testicles and penis grow just as fingers and legs, and eyes grow. Girls and women do not have these parts of the body.

The testicles are not ready to make fully grown sperm cells until a boy is about 13 or 14 years old. Then his body also makes a whitish liquid which the sperm cells need to swim in from one place to another. The liquid and the sperm cells together are called *semen* (SEE-men). Semen passes out of the body through the penis only at certain times. This can occur only when the penis is firm and erect instead of soft and limp, as it is most of the time.

Now you can see how wonderfully God made the boy's body as well as the girl's. The girl's organs that equip her to be a mother are safely on the inside of her body. It is here that the baby is protected while it grows until it is ready to be born. The boy's organs that equip him to be a father are on the outside of the body. The

Where Did You Come From?

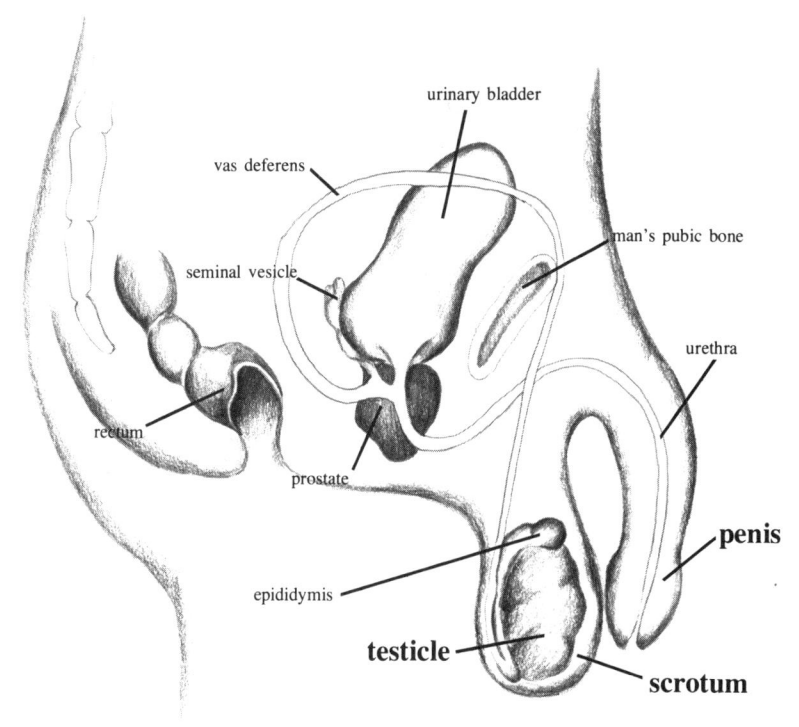

boy is usually stronger and more active, and his organs, although very tender if squeezed, are not as delicate as the girls. Even so, we must be very careful not to kick or hit girls in the abdomen, and not to kick or hit the boys between the legs—for it could be very painful and might even damage these parts of our body.

A Story of Love—How the Sperm Cell Meets the Egg Cell

How does the sperm cell make its way from the father's body into the mother's body and merge with the egg cell? The answer is part of the story of the love of your father and mother for each other.

Surely you can name many ways your father and

LET'S TALK ABOUT LIFE

mother show their love to each other. Perhaps they give each other gifts at Christmas or on birthdays. Maybe your daddy gives your mother something special on Mother's Day. Your mother cooks things your father likes to eat, and sometimes your father takes your mother out at night for entertainment. Maybe you've seen your mother put her arms around your father, or perhaps you've seen your father hug and kiss your mother. When Christian people love each other enough to marry, there is a deep attraction for each other. They like to be in each other's presence. They like to be close to each other.

Sometimes a mother's and father's love takes on a special quality. At times like this they want to be alone, and want to be very close to each other in an act called "mating" or "sexual intercourse." When they lie close together in bed in a loving embrace, the father's penis sometimes becomes erect and can fit into the mother's vagina. After a few minutes of being very close, the father's semen can then flow from the penis into the mother's vagina. The sperm cells swim deep into the vagina, enter the uterus and go up into the tubes. The mother, of course, cannot "feel" the sperm moving up to find an egg cell.

If there is an egg cell ready in the mother's body, a sperm cell can move through the egg's covering and make a fertilized egg cell. Only one sperm cell can unite, or join, with the egg. This is called "fertilizing" the egg. If an egg is fertilized, it then moves down into the uterus where it stays while it is growing into a baby. However, sperm cells do not meet an egg every time they enter a mother's vagina; for remember, an egg cell is released from an ovary only once a month and can

Where Did You Come From?

be "fertilized" only during a two- or three-day period before the egg leaves the mother's body.

Once the sperm cell has united with the egg cell in

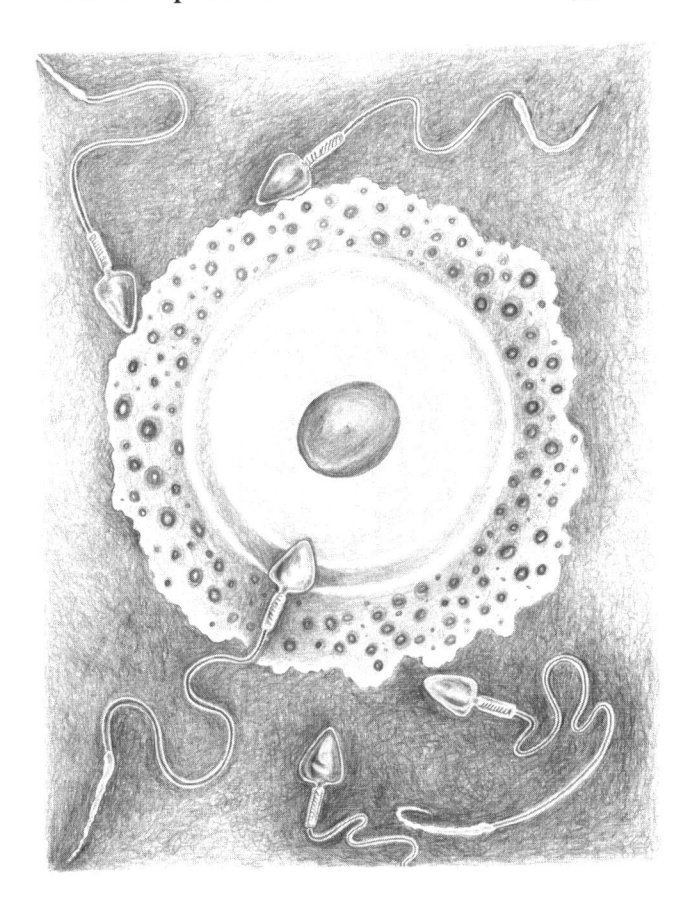

the mother's tubes, the new cell moves into the uterus—and grows there for nine months. The moment the two cells unite is called *conception* (kon-sep-shun), and from then until the baby's born the mother is spoken of as being *pregnant* (preg-nant). No more eggs will be produced in the mother's body until after the baby is born. In fact, this is the first sign the mother will have that she is pregnant, because her monthly cycle of producing new egg cells will stop.

Nine months is a long time, isn't it? But the egg and the sperm are so small that it takes a long time for them to become a baby with eyes, ears, nose, mouth, arms, legs, stomach, skin, bones and everything else. Nine months is really a very *short* time for all that to happen.

So you see, this new life is created in love. God is love, the Bible says, and when He allows married men and women to create a new life He wants them to do it by becoming as much like Him as they can—by being filled with love. This is what the mother and father in a Christian home are doing when they lie very close to each other in bed—they are telling each other how much they love God and how much they love one another.

This closeness brings a great deal of pleasure to the mother and father of a Christian home. It is God's way of allowing them to show their great love to each other. Sometimes men and women (even older boys and girls) who are not married lie closely in bed with each other. This is called *fornication* and is forbidden by God in many places in the Bible—"For this is the will of God...that ye should abstain from fornication" (1 Thessalonians 4:2). This special pleasure and act of love and devotion is to be reserved only for men and women after marriage—after they have vowed to God and to each other that they will love each other in this special way and will never love anybody else in this special way

Where Did You Come From?

until they are separated by death.

Now remember, the Bible says that when two people are married, they should have sexual intercourse. It is God's wonderful way of allowing them to show their love for each other—not only because it gives them both pleasure, but because this is how the two of them become one. It is at this time that married people learn to *know* their deepest love for each other. In fact, that is the word the Bible uses. "And Adam knew Eve his wife; and she conceived, and bare Cain and said, 'I have gotten a man from the Lord' " (Genesis 4:1). However, when young people are not willing to wait until marriage to show their love for each other as God has commanded them to do, then they feel guilty and want to hide from God—and sometimes babies are born without having a home to live in. Remember: God's highest purpose in allowing a mother and father to have sexual intercourse was to let the sperm cell from the father unite with the egg cell from the mother and make a new life—a baby who would be raised in a loving Christian home.

LET'S TALK ABOUT LIFE

TRUE OR FALSE: (mark T or F)

____ It takes both a man and a woman to have a baby.

____ Mothers are supposed to love babies more than fathers.

____ The egg cell comes from the father's body.

____ Sperm cells look like little tadpoles.

____ The girl's sexual organs are inside her body.

____ It takes more than a year for a baby to develop inside the mother.

____ Boys and girls should not have sexual intercourse until they are married.

CHAPTER THREE

The Baby Grows Inside the Mother

The Baby Grows Inside the Mother

How the baby grows in the uterus

How the mother's body helps the baby grow

After the mother becomes pregnant, special care must be taken to make sure the mother and new baby will be healthy when the baby is born. During these nine months the mother should visit a doctor regularly. He will tell her what she should eat and will listen for the baby's heart beat by placing a *stethoscope* (STETH-uh-skope) against the mother's abdomen. As the baby grows larger in her body she will see the doctor more frequently.

The doctor is the mother's good friend during this time, and he will suggest ways she can help the baby be well and healthy when it is born. Most mothers who work (outside the home as teachers, librarians, in stores, or at jobs) are able to keep working right up until just before the time the baby is born.

For the last few months before the baby is born, a mother may wear different clothes which are made to

LET'S TALK ABOUT LIFE

fit her growing body. Such dresses are called "maternity dresses" because *maternity* (muh-TUR-ni-tee) means motherhood. You have probably seen women wearing such clothes at church, in the store, or maybe even at a ball game.

This is usually an exciting time around the home. The mother and other members of the family start getting the new baby's clothes and diapers ready, even before he is born. If this is the first baby they will do a lot of shopping, buying things like baby cribs, diapers, bottles, maybe a car seat, playpen or even a baby carriage. If there have been other children in the family, they will already have many of these things, but they may still have to buy new diapers and get the house ready for the new baby. Sometimes older brothers and sisters can help to paint or repair the old baby furniture or toys that they used when they were babies. It is fun for the family to do these things together, so the baby will have what he needs.

How the Baby Grows in the Uterus

While the mother and the rest of the family are busy getting ready for the baby, the baby is busy getting ready to be born. He keeps on growing and growing, safe inside his mother's body. At first, of course, he doesn't look like a baby at all. In the beginning he is simply a fertilized cell, too small even to be seen. But soon that cell divides so there are four cells. Each cell divides again, making eight. The cells keep on dividing. As new cells are made, the baby grows.

Before the cells have divided many times, this little mass of cells begins to actually look like a human being. It is attached to the wall of the uterus and is drawing nourishment from the mother's body. As the cells

The Baby Grows Inside the Mother

keep on dividing, they begin to form different parts of the baby's body, such as the lungs, stomach, bones, muscles, skin, sex organs, and other parts.

At the end of two months the baby begins to look more

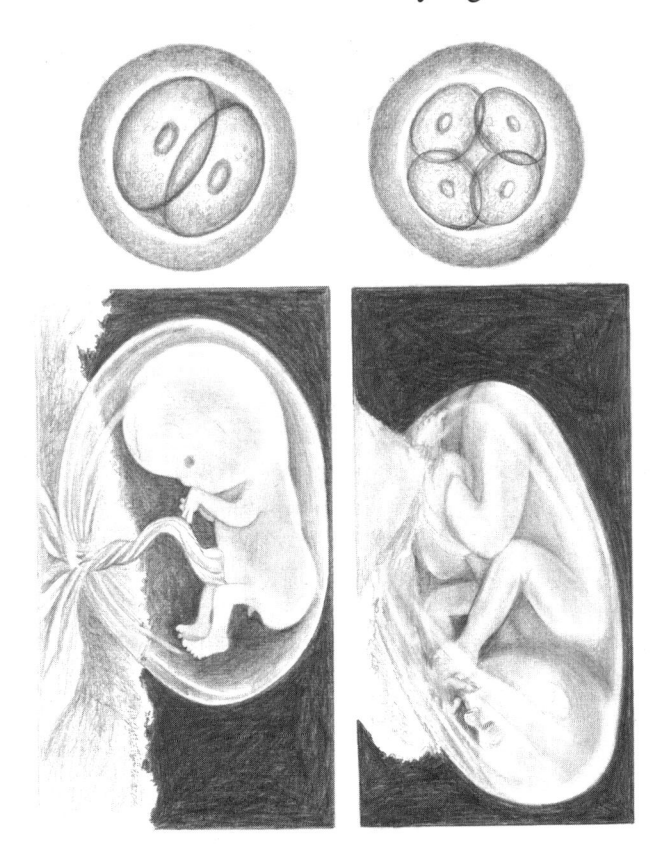

like a baby, although a rather odd one. It is about an inch long, with a head about as big as his body. It has very tiny arms and legs and has eyes, ears, nose and mouth. By the third month of growth, the baby is three or four inches long and soon after this he can move his arms and legs. When the mother feels these movements, she is happy to know the new baby is growing normally. By the end of the fourth month, the baby is probably a foot long and weighs about one pound. By now he is beginning to kick his legs against the inside of his mother's uterus.

At six months, the unborn baby looks more as he will after he is born, but he is still not fully developed. He needs to stay inside the mother where he is warm, protected, and fed. He is not ready to live outside his mother because the organs inside his body are not ready. His skin may be wrinkled because he doesn't have the padding of fat that will make him plump and help keep him warm after birth. In the next three months he will grow much faster.

By the end of the ninth month, when the baby is ready to be born, he weighs six or seven pounds and is about 21 inches long. Originally much smaller than the head of a pin, the egg and sperm have grown into a strong, squirming, lovable human baby.

You may wonder how there can possibly be room in a mother's body for a seven-pound baby. If you could see an unborn baby you would find that God has expertly packaged him, with arms and legs comfortably folded close to his body, to fit into as small a space as possible.

How the Mother's Body Helps the Baby Grow

During the nine months in his mother's body, the baby is not only well protected, but well fed. Soon after the fertilized egg attaches itself to the uterus, a sac grows around it. The sac is filled with a warm protective water-

The Baby Grows Inside the Mother

like fluid and the baby floats safely in this fluid-filled sac. This protects him from small jolts and bumps that

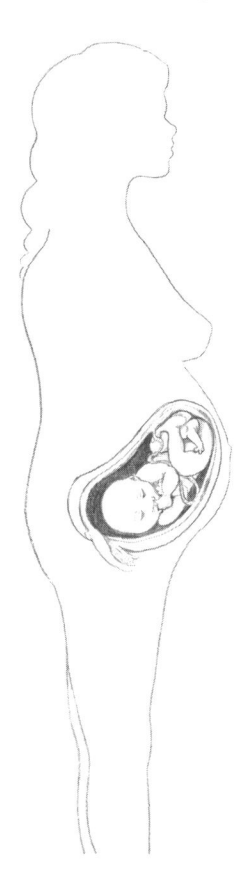

otherwise might harm him.

The baby can live in this fluid while he is in his mother's body because he does not breathe through his nose nor eat through his mouth. There is a special arrangement by which the mother's blood brings him food that he needs and the part of the air he must have in order to live. This part of the air is called *oxygen* (OX-uh-jin).

A tube called the *umbilical* (um-BIL-i-kal) cord is attached to the baby's abdomen at the place where his *navel* (na-vel) will be. The navel is sometimes called the "belly-button." The other end of this soft tube is attached to the side of the mother's uterus at a place where there is a special network of blood vessels. Here the mother's blood vessels and the baby's are close together. The network is called the *placenta* (pla-SEN-tuh). Think of the umbilical cord as a small pipeline. Through it, some of the baby's blood vessels run into the placenta. The mother's blood does not flow through the baby or mix with its blood. Instead, digested food and oxygen flow from the mother's blood into the baby's blood and allow the baby to grow. The waste materials that collect in the baby's blood pass the other way, through the umbilical cord (pipeline) into the mother's bloodstream, and her body gets rid of them just as it rids itself of its own waste and leftover materials.

The mother, you see, is actually living two lives—one is her own, and the other is the life of the little baby who is depending on her for its oxygen and food and elimination of waste products. Mothers who are expecting a baby like to say they are "eating for two." You can see that she is also breathing for two and getting rid of waste material for two—herself and the baby.

The mother's body is always capable of taking care of the baby that God has allowed to grow inside of her if she keeps healthy. The uterus enlarges while the baby is growing. Sometimes there are two babies in the mother's uterus at the same time. When this happens,

The Baby Grows Inside the Mother

we call the babies twins, and the mother's uterus becomes big enough to take care of both of them.

It is no wonder that everyone in the family thinks that this is a very important time in the mother's life. Most fathers think that their wives are the most beautiful when they are pregnant. If you will look at the face of a woman who is pregnant, you will see that her eyes often sparkle and her face shines as if God Himself has touched her. And indeed, He may have. Seldom does God come as close to a human being as when He lets a mother bring a new life into the world.

The Bible teaches us that God is not only the Creator of life, but that through Jesus Christ He gives "new life" to those who accept Him. Jesus Himself talked about the wondrous miracle of salvation in terms of a mother giving birth to a child. He said that salvation is so wonderful that it is like being "born again." If Jesus said that salvation is like being born (and the Bible says that salvation is the most wonderful spiritual thing that can happen to a person), then think how wonderful birth must be.

TRUE OR FALSE (Answer T or F)

____ A pregnant mother must stay in bed all the time.

____ The new baby is not "alive" until it is born.

____ The new baby lives in fluid while in its mother's tummy.

____ The mother's blood feeds the new baby until it is born.

CHAPTER FOUR
The Baby Is Born

The Baby Is Born

The mother helps with the birth

After living nine months in the mother's womb (or uterus), the baby is ready to live on its own, apart from its mother. Some babies are born after only seven or eight months in the womb. They are called *premature* (pree-ma-TYOOR) babies, or "premies" (pree-mees). They may require special medical care in the hospital for several weeks after birth because they are underweight and not fully developed.

The Mother Helps With the Birth

When the baby's birth is near, something interesting happens. The mother's uterus has been enlarging for a long time, but finally it stops getting bigger. Instead, the muscles of the uterus begin to push the baby out and into the vagina—the passageway that leads to the outside world.

When the muscles of the uterus start contracting (flexing) and pushing the baby out, the mother feels cramps,

LET'S TALK ABOUT LIFE

something like a mild muscle cramp.

This is called *labor* (LAY-bor), and the cramping sensations are called *labor pains*. Usually she hurries to a hospital, where the doctors and nurses can assist her in the birth of the baby. If she is going to a hospital to have the baby, she probably has packed a suitcase ahead of time with everything she will need.

By the last weeks of pregnancy, the baby has usually turned until it lies head down in the uterus. The baby's head is the first part of the body to be pushed into the mother's vagina. The vagina stretches quite a lot so that it is big enough for the baby to pass through. The sac of fluid around the baby will probably break after the mother's labor pains begin. God knows that it is time for the baby to leave the warmth and protection of its mother's womb and to make its entrance into the world. Before long the baby comes out into the world and not long afterward, the placenta comes out too. Immediately the mother's body begins to return to normal, as the uterus starts shrinking back to its normal size.

Sometimes it takes only a few moments, but sometimes it takes many hours for a baby to be born. The doctor may give the mother some medicine to make her comfortable if the labor is hard enough so that she needs it. When the mother holds the baby in her arms she is so happy to see the little boy or girl that she tends to forget all about the time of labor.

When the baby is just born, the umbilical cord still connects the baby's body to the placenta. The doctor ties and cuts the unbilical cord near the baby's body. Since there are no nerves in the cord, cutting it does not hurt the baby nor the mother. When the opening at the end of the cord has sealed and healed, the stub

The Baby Is Born

of the umbilical cord drops off. The mark or depression that remains on the abdomen is called the navel, or the "belly button."

Just about the first thing the baby does when he comes out into the world is cry. The doctor and nurses are happy to hear the baby cry, because they know that it has begun to breathe with its own lungs. Through its own lungs the baby must take in the oxygen for its body's needs; it cannot depend on its mother for food and oxygen. Sometimes the doctor has to give the baby a little spank on the bottom to make it start crying. This sometimes seems cruel, but it may be necessary, for crying helps the baby off to a healthy start in life. In fact, the more the baby cries when he is born, the more he exercises his lungs—which is good for him. You may think your little baby brother or sister cries an awful lot, but this may be just a sign that he has healthy lungs.

The mother may choose to feed the baby regular milk (cow's milk) from a bottle. However, many mothers choose to feed the baby the way God originally provided, from her breasts. Milk flows from inside the breasts through openings in the nipples. When the baby sucks on them he is able to get warm fresh milk. The breasts have been preparing to make plenty of milk while the mother has been carrying the baby in her abdomen, and they will make fresh milk as long as the baby nurses. Once he stops nursing, the milk will no longer be made in the mother's breasts. This is just another example of God's wonderful way of providing for the new baby. The milk from the mother's breast is just the right temperature and the perfect formula. Besides, the baby has a natural instinct to suck. Maybe you've seen a baby sucking on a pacifier or on his thumb or fingers. God has given him this instinct, just as He has given the mother milk, so he will not go hungry.

Most mothers and fathers want to have the baby born in the hospital. Doctors and nurses have everything there they need to take the best care of the mother and her newly born child. The mother is taken into a special room called a delivery room for the birth of the baby. The father may wait outside in another room, waiting and praying for the mother, the doctors and the nurses, as well as the new baby.

Newborn babies are usually pinkish red and quite funny looking, but to the mother and father their new baby is the most beautiful thing they've ever seen. Immediately after the baby is born, the nurse gives him his first bath and then lets the mother see him, if she is awake, and hold him in her arms. What a glad moment this is for her!

It's a happy day when the mother and baby come home from the hospital. Of course, the mother may need to rest more than usual after she comes home, and the new baby needs special care. But the doctor and nurse will tell the family how to look after both of them.

All the new baby can do is eat and sleep and cry and wet his diapers. But everyone loves him, especially his father and mother, who are the two people responsible for letting God take their two cells and form them together to create the new baby.

No wonder King David wrote many years ago, "I will praise thee; for I am fearfully and wonderfully made..." (Psalm 139:14).

The Baby Is Born

FILL IN THE BLANK

1. How long did you live in your mother's body?__
   _____

2. Where were you born?_____

3. Did you cry a lot when you were born? Ask your mother or father. Yes____ No____.

4. Did you nurse at your mother's breast? Yes____ No____. If you did, how long? _____
   _____

5. Ask your mother and father to describe what happened when you were born.

CHAPTER FIVE
Girl or Boy?

Girl or Boy?

When I was 5 years old, my mother and daddy announced one day that they were going to bring a baby sister home to live with us. The four boys in the family were thrilled, and we all took turns picking names until we decided on one upon which we could all agree. How did we know for sure that Mother and Daddy were going to bring home a baby girl? Because they were *adopting* a daughter. Instead of having any more children the usual way, they found a baby that had been born to a mother who couldn't take care of her—and they adopted the baby as their own. This way they knew they were getting a sister to go with the four brothers who already lived in the big house in Florida. Adopting a baby is one way a mother and daddy can be absolutely sure whether they'll get a boy or a girl.

But there is another way that parents can sometimes tell whether they will have a boy or a girl. Doctors can use a special microphone-like instrument to take a "picture"—similar to an X-ray—of the baby while still inside the mother's body. This is called a *sonogram* (SAWN-uh-gram). A sonogram is made with sound waves and shows the outline of the baby. By looking at this outline, the doctor can sometimes tell if the baby will be a boy or a girl. A sonogram is most often used to show doctors the position of the baby—or if there is more than one baby—but it will sometimes show the sex of the baby, too.

All this adds to the excitement of having a new baby in the house, though. Many parents pick out two sets of names—a boy's name and a girl's name. Since pink is supposed to be a girl's color and blue a boy's color, many parents wait until after the baby is born to buy things for baby's room or to buy clothes.

Sometimes a big sister or big brother in the family will decide he wants a little sister—or a little brother. Then, when the baby comes and is not what they want, they pout and act very angry. But the mother and daddy are happy, whatever it is. They just take what comes! Have you ever wondered why some babies turn out to be boys and others to be girls?

There are two kinds of sperm cells. One kind will produce a baby girl if it fertilizes the egg; the other kind will produce a baby boy. There are equal numbers of each kind. So you see, there is a 50-50 chance that the baby will be a boy and a 50-50 chance that it will be a girl. It depends on which kind of sperm has fertilized the egg.

Again we can see God's handiwork in all that we do. What if only one out of five sperm cells was a potential "girl" cell? That would mean that there would probably

Girl or Boy?

be four times as many boys as girls. Or what if it were the other way around and there were four times as many girls as boys? But God had all this figured out when He made us, so we have about as many girls as we have boys.

After the new baby arrives, friends and visitors at the hospital or in the home will stand around the baby's crib and try to decide whether the baby looks like the father or the mother. "He has his father's nose," someone says. Grandmother says, "He looks just like his daddy did when he was a baby," and the kid across the street, looking in over the top of the crib, says, "Boy, he sure is ugly, isn't he?"

You see, everybody thinks the baby ought to look like someone—that is, almost everybody. Sometimes visitors in your home may look at you and make remarks about who you look like. Perhaps you wish they wouldn't. But you yourself have wondered, haven't you, what makes a child look like his father or mother or some other member of the family?

The fertilized egg from which you grew was made when your father's sperm cell united with your mother's egg cell. No wonder, then, that you look like your mother, or your father, or some other member of your family.

Through the sperm cell and the egg cell, family traits such as color of eyes or hair, or the shape of nose, ears or other features are passed along from parents to children. This is the reason brothers and sisters often look alike although each is a different person.

In fact, no person in the world is exactly like you. Each person is different, although you may look very much like your mother or father.

LET'S TALK ABOUT LIFE

Tall parents are likely to have tall children, and short parents often have short children. But this is not always the case. I bet you know of some parents who are very short but who have a great big tall son. The family traits that are passed on from parents to child are said to be the child's *heredity* (hehr-ED-i-tee).

Sometimes children look more like their grandparents, or an aunt or an uncle, than like their parents. And sometimes they don't look like anyone in the family! This is not surprising, because the combination of traits you can inherit, or receive, is so great. Remember, half of what you are comes from your father and half from your mother. These mixtures can be combined in all sorts of ways. Your parents got their family traits from your grandparents and so on, back down the line of relatives.

The only case when brothers and sisters look exactly alike is when one fertilized egg grows into two or more babies, instead of one baby. If there are two babies, they are called "identical twins" or "like twins" because they come from the same fertilized egg. They are always of the same sex. They look so much alike that it is almost impossible to tell them apart.

On a rare occasion there may be two egg cells released by the mother at the same time, and a different sperm cell unites with each one. Then two babies grow in the uterus at once, but in this case, each one has a different heredity. These are "unlike" twins or "non-identical" twins. They do not look any more alike than most brothers and sisters do. One can be a girl, and one a boy—or both can be boys, or both girls. In the United States, twins occur once in about every 88 births. Only one fourth of these sets of twins are identical.

Girl or Boy?

One thing about heredity we need to remember: Human egg cells and sperm cells always make human beings. Human parents have human babies. A male and female dog have puppies, a male and female cat have kittens, and so on. It is impossible for it to happen otherwise. Aren't you glad? Think how horrible it would be if your mother went to the hospital to have a baby, and instead brought home a baby alligator and said it was your brother.

But this is all part of God's wonderful plan. When God created the earth he said, "Let the earth bring forth the living creature *after his kind*, cattle, and creeping thing, and beast of the earth *after his kind*: and it was so" (Genesis 1:24). Just as each animal was a special creation of God and could give birth only to his own kind, so man is God's highest creation and can give birth only to another human being.

Human beings are God's special creation. All other living animals have babies too, but none of them is able to care for them as well as a human mother and father can care for their baby.

Many animals have babies the same way that human beings do. Those that do are called mammals. The male animal places the sperm cells inside the mother's body by inserting his penis into her vagina. The fertilized egg cell grows into a baby inside the mother's uterus, and the baby comes out through the vagina at birth. The mother animal also supplies milk for the baby from her breasts, called "mammary glands." Many mother animals care for their young and protect them from danger.

Animals are different from humans in some very important ways. You may have wondered why animals such as cats and dogs have so many babies at once, while human mothers usually have only one baby at a time. In many female animals there are likely to be several eggs released at one time, so more than one egg is fertilized at the same time.

There are other differences too. Animals do not choose their mates because they love them. A male cat may mate with any female cat he sees. He does not stay with the female cat after they have mated to help her look after the kittens after they are born. In fact he would not even know his own kittens if he saw them. Even the mother cat does not look after them for more than a few weeks. The father bird is a much better father than the father cat, for at least he stays around to help feed the baby birds after they are hatched.

It's a different story when human beings make a home, for human beings are the only "animals" that have the breath of God in them. In the beginning God said, "Let us make man in our image, after our likeness..." (Genesis 1:26). Man is very different from the animals, for only man is made in the image of God. God gave man the ability to know about God and to choose to love Him.

Girl or Boy?

FILL IN THE BLANK

1. Are "adopted" children loved as much as children born to the parents? Yes____ No____.
2. Do you wish you were a boy____ girl____? Why?
   _____
3. Whom do others say you look like? Your father____, your mother____, both____, your grandfather____, your grandmother____, your brother____, your sister____, your aunt____, your uncle____.
4. Do you think you will grow up to be taller____, shorter____ than your mom or dad?

CHAPTER SIX
Growing Up

Growing Up

Getting taller

Getting stronger

What is the earliest thing you can remember when you look back over your whole life? The very first thing I can remember is stacking two wooden crates on top of each other behind the house and trying to stand on them so I could look through a window. The crates fell down, and so did I—hitting my head against the side of the house. When I put my hand on the hurt place, it was sticky with blood. My mother cut all the hair away from the little cut and dabbed it with iodine—which hurt more than hitting it against the side of the house. That's the very first thing I can remember.

The very second thing I can remember is the time the woods caught on fire beside our big new house out in the country. The fire was burning on two sides of the house, and all the men came running in out of the orange grove to help put the fire out. The fire trucks came, and while some of them squirted water on the fire, others squirted water on the roof of our brand new house so it wouldn't catch fire. My daddy made all the children go in the house, and get on their knees, and pray that God would make the wind blow in the other direction so it wouldn't burn our house down. I can remember kneeling beside my little brother, smelling smoke, and hearing the men outside shouting and fighting the fire. I prayed and cried at the same time. I can also remember Daddy running into the house and telling us all to come outside, that God had answered our prayers. The wind had shifted, and the fire was moving away from the house rather than toward it. Those are the very first and the very second things I can remember as a little boy. Now what can you remember?

Probably you cannot remember very much that happened before you were 3 years old. Nearly everyone forgets the earliest things that happened in his young life. Sometimes the only things we can remember are the things our parents told us about. Some of the stories your parents have told you are probably funny, because little babies often do funny things. Some of them may seem silly to you. Just the same, it is fun to have your parents remember these little things about you because it shows that you are very important to them and that they love you.

If you look at snapshots of yourself as a baby, sometimes you can scarcely believe that you are the same person. Many parents have pictures of themselves when they were babies, and it seems strange that your mother and daddy were ever that small. My wife and I had pictures taken of each of our five children when they were 1 year old. These pictures are hanging on the wall of our bedroom and sometimes our children—now grown—

Growing Up

come in, look at them, and giggle. Isn't it funny the way we grow up? Look how much you have grown since you were a baby. Not only are you much taller and heavier, but you have grown up in other interesting ways that we are going to talk about in this chapter.

Remember, in all these ways your parents helped you grow up. They have given you the food your body needs for growth. They have given you a home where you can work and play, sleep and rest. They have helped you learn many things about the world around you. They have sent you to school and have taken you to church. Maybe your parents even taught you how to pray, and have read Bible stories to you. If you tried to make a list of all the ways in which they have helped you grow up, it would be a long, long list.

But your parents haven't done it all. The Spirit of God has been close to you all the years while you were growing up. God has sent His protecting angels to keep you from harm. The Bible says that the boy Jesus not only grew, but that He was under the special protection of God while He *did* grow. "And the child grew, and waxed strong in spirit, filled with wisdom: and the grace of God was upon him" (Luke 2:40). God has been watching over you, too.

So you see, your parents are not the only ones who have helped you grow up. Grandparents have helped, and Sunday school teachers, and preachers, and school teachers, and friends in the town where you live. All have helped you grow up. So has God. And then you have done a great deal of your own growing up too.

Getting Taller

Have you ever wondered why you grow taller? There must be something inside you that makes you spurt up.

LET'S TALK ABOUT LIFE

Have you ever wanted to be taller than you are? Remember the times when you were measured beside one of your playmates or your brother or sister, and you stretched and stretched your neck like a giraffe or goose, trying to be taller than you were? Too bad we can't make ourselves taller just by wanting to be taller, isn't it? But God says that growing taller is left up to Him.

In the Sermon on the Mount, Jesus asks a funny question just to show that we can't do this ourselves. He asks: "Can any of you, however much he worries, make himself an inch taller" (Matthew 6:27, Phillips)? No, you grow taller the same way you grew in your mother's womb, by your body cells dividing and making new cells. You can stunt your growth by not standing up straight or by eating improper foods—but basically your height is something you cannot control.

You grow taller when the long bones in your legs grow longer, and the bones in your back, neck and head grow bigger. Both before and after you are born, your bones grow in two ways. They get bigger, and they become harder.

Some bones of little babies are soft because they have not formed into real bone yet. They are called *cartilage* (KAR-ti-luj). One of the places you still have cartilage is in your ear. Take your fingers and wiggle your ear around. See? It is hard but it is not as hard as the bone right beside it in your head. Babies' bones are mostly the soft variety, as you have in your ears.

When the baby is ready to be born, some of his bones have become hard in some places. The bones in his head, however, especially in the top of his head, are still soft. This makes it easier for his head to pass through his mother's vagina.

Growing Up

After the baby is born, it takes a long time for all the cartilage to change into strong, hard bones. You will be about old enough to go to college or take a job before all the changes in your bones are completed. This is the reason you should eat lots of good bone-building foods—like milk, which is rich in *calcium* (KAL-see-um), a mineral that makes your bones hard. Boys and girls who eat lots of fresh vegetables, meats and milk will have strong bones and hard teeth.

The bones of your legs, feet, arms, and hands, are called "long bones," because of their shape. The drumstick of a chicken has the shape of a long bone. The next time you eat all the meat off the drumstick, look at the shape of the bone. It has a long, slim part in the middle that is called a "shaft," and a wider part at the end that is called "head." There is a layer of cartilage between the shaft and the head. Growth in length takes place in this layer of cartilage which becomes hard bone as you grow older and eat the right foods.

The cartilage in the shaft gradually turns into hard bone, and some hard places form in the head or end of the bone. At the same time, new cartilage grows in the cartilage layer at the end of the shaft. This goes on for years, and during all this time, the bone can keep on growing in length. At the same time that the bone grows longer, it grows thicker by adding new bones around the outside.

Finally, no more new cartilage is formed in the layer between the shaft and the head of the bone. After that, the shaft and the head grow firmly together and the bone stops growing in length.

Growth in height, caused by growth in the length of bones, usually stops when you are between 16 and the early 20s. You may be an "early grower." Or, like some, you may be a "late grower." You just might remain short until you are in high school and then, for no understandable reason, shoot up until you are taller than anyone else in school. All these ways of growing are normal, and God knows which is best for each boy and girl. Girls usually reach full height a couple of years sooner than boys of the same age, but boys usually pass them by the time they are in the ninth grade and go on to grow even taller.

Do you remember the term "heredity"? Remember we said it has to do with the parts of the egg cell and the sperm cell that created you in the very beginning? Heredity has much to do with your height. If you are tall, medium, or short, as a little tot, you are likely to be tall, medium, or short when you are an adult. During the years when boys and girls have their spurt of fast growing, you may feel mixed up about your height. One year you may be shorter than all your playmates and the next year taller. Sometimes a girl will sprout up and be very tall and skinny and tower above all her playmates. But in a couple of years they will catch up with her—and some of them might even grow taller than she is.

Bones are not the only parts of your body that are growing. There are other parts of your body that are growing too. Some of these are your muscles. Muscles are the parts of your body that make you move. Before you were old enough to go to kindergarten, your muscles were much smaller and weaker than they are now. In fact, when you were born, they made up only about one-fourth of your weight. By the time you started to school, your muscles had started growing bigger and stronger.

Growing Up

By the time you are about 12 years old, your muscles will make up about one-half of your body weight.

Have you seen pictures of strong men pulling their arms up and making a fist and showing the big muscles in their upper arm near their shoulder? Why don't you try it and see if you have a big muscle? The tighter you draw your arm up, the harder and larger the muscle grows. Now try something else. Straighten your arm out all the way and make a tight fist. Now with your other hand feel the bottom side of that arm. See, there are muscles down there too. The muscles on the top of your arm help pull your hand up. The muscles on the bottom of your arm pull the hand down. Your body is full of such muscles.

Try something else. Put your hand on the side of your face just under and in front of your ear. Press lightly. Now put your back teeth together and clench tightly. Do you feel that big knot that forms under your skin? That is the muscle that works your jaw and helps you talk and chew your food. You probably use that muscle a lot, don't you?

The older you grow, and the more you exercise your muscles by bending them back and forth, the stronger you get. Naturally you are much stronger now than you were when you were in kindergarten. Can you guess how much stronger the grip in your hand is, at 11 years, than it was when you were 6 years old? It is just about twice as strong.

Many other parts of your body could be mentioned in this chapter on getting stronger. For example, your heart pumps blood through your body night and day. Your heart is a muscle, and like all muscles, the more it works the stronger it gets—that is, if you take good care of it. Every minute of your life, your blood carries food and oxygen to all your body cells and takes waste material from them. As the cells carry on their work and make new cells, your body grows. Your stomach, heart, lungs, head, skin, bones, muscles, and nerves—all of them—grow. Sometimes, one part of your body grows faster than another, and so you may have very long legs and very large feet. But as you grow older God allows the different part of your body to catch up with the other parts.

Our bodies are wonderfully made. In fact, they are the most wonderful things that God has ever made. The apostle Paul liked to write about the body, sometimes comparing it with the way people ought to live together. Read what he had to say about your body.

"Our bodies have many parts, but the many parts make only one body when they are all put together.... Yes, the body has many parts, not just one part. If the foot says, 'I am not a part of the body because I am not a hand,' that does not make it any less a part of the body. And what would you think if you heard an ear say, 'I am not part of the body because I am only an ear, and not an eye?' Would that make it any less a part of the body? Suppose the whole body were an eye—then how would you hear? Or if your whole body were just one big ear, how would you smell anything? But that isn't the way God has made us. He has made many parts for our bodies and has put each part just where he wants it. What a strange thing a body would be if it had only one part. So he had made many parts, but still there is only one body. The eye can never say to the hand, 'I don't need you.' The hand can't say to the feet, 'I don't need you.' And some of the parts that seem weakest and

Growing Up

least important are really the most necessary.

"Yes, we are especially glad to have some parts that seem rather odd! And we carefully protect from the eyes of others those parts that should not be seen, while of course the parts that may be seen do not require this special care. So God has put the body together in such a way that extra honor and care are given to those parts that might otherwise seem less important. This makes for happiness among the parts, so that the parts have the same care for each other that they do for themselves. If one part suffers, all the parts suffer with it, and if one part is honored, all the parts are glad" (1 Corinthians 12:12, 14-26, *Living Letters*).

The Bible also says that this body of ours is not our own. It belongs to God, and He has just loaned it to us. It needs to be well cared for. Paul says, "Haven't you yet learned that your body is the home of the Holy Spirit God gave you, and that he lives within you? Your own body does not belong to you. For God has bought you with a great price. So use every part of your body to give glory back to God, because he owns it" (1 Corinthians 6:18-20, *Living Letters*).

LET'S TALK ABOUT LIFE

FILL IN THE BLANK

1. What are the very first things you can remember?
   _____
   _____ .

2. List some ways your parents have helped you grow up? _____
   _____

3. What is the longest bone in your body? _____

4. Who grows faster as a young child?
   Girls_____ Boys_____.

5. What muscle pumps the blood through your body?

6. Who owns your body?
   Me_____, my parents_____, God_____.

CHAPTER SEVEN
Growing and Learning

Growing and Learning

Feelings grow up too

Even friendships change as you grow

Have you ever tried to count how many things you have learned since you were born? If you counted every separate thing you have learned, there would be thousands of them. Many of the things, well, really, most of the things you have learned to do you weren't even aware you were learning.

A newborn baby cannot sit up, or stand, or feed himself, or control his bowel movements, or talk. He cannot even reach for something and pick it up. He can't even focus his eyes on anything at first. One of the first things a baby learns to do is to look at his hands. He doesn't even know they are there until one day he waves them in front of his face and WOW! "What's that?" he says. After that he will spend long minutes just looking at his hands. Some months later he will be able to grab at things with his hand and still later learn to pick things up between his thumb and fingers.

LET'S TALK ABOUT LIFE

You can probably think of dozens of things that a little baby learns by seeing, hearing, tasting, smelling, and touching. For example, he learns about his bottle of milk by seeing it and getting used to the taste of the milk as he drinks it. Later, he learns how to swallow solid food—and how to chew. But he has to *learn* all these things. The first time your mother put something into your mouth for you to chew up—you spit it out.

By feeling and touching, the baby learns about things that are smooth and things that are rough. He learns about the sharp edges of his blocks and the roundness of his ball, the softness of his pillow or the hardness of the end of his bed when he bumps his head against it. He learns about his body, too, through his sense of touch.

By the time two or three years have passed, the little child can walk, run, jump a little, climb up and down stairs, throw things in a funny sort of way, jabber and use new words, and maybe even ride a tricycle. A little later he can put on most of his clothes by himself (although he sometimes gets them on upside down and inside out), and he has even learned to go to the bathroom by himself.

When he was a little baby, his nerves and his muscles were not ready for him to do these things. Even if you hold a very young baby so his feet touch the floor, he cannot walk, because his nerves and muscles are not grown-up enough for walking. Besides, his bones are not strong enough to support him, and if you forced him to walk too soon it could make his bones bend (remember, they are still soft and won't get hard until much later).

Crawling strengthens a baby's muscles without injur-

Growing and Learning

ing his bones. And one day the baby will pull himself up, and then, before long, he will be standing alone in the middle of the floor. Then he will go PLOP! and sit back down. But all the time his muscles and bones are getting stronger and stronger until one day he will take his first step. After that it isn't long before he is running all over the house.

It seems that growing and learning go together. Boys and girls of your age can run, jump, swim, skate, and throw a ball. You can play any number of games better than first-graders, for example. You can easily do arithmetic problems (well, almost easily, anyway) and you can do the kind of school work too hard for you when you were in the first grade. In fact, you can even read this little book—which is something that would have been impossible several years ago. This is because you have been growing up in mind and body and you are able to learn new and harder things as you grow.

Learning New Words

If there is a baby in your home, you know how excited the older members of the family are when he says his first words. It is just as exciting as when he takes his first steps. His first baby words are the beginning of his language, which he will need all his life. When he starts to school, he will learn to read and write words as well as speak them.

It is very important that you learn the right words to describe things that you do and see and learn about. Some of the most important words in our language are the words that describe your body correctly. However, since some of these words are hard to pronounce, your mother and father will let you use easier words while you are a baby. Instead of saying "urinate," you may use

LET'S TALK ABOUT LIFE

words such as "tinkle" or "wee-wee." These are usually family words, and each family will probably use different words. You can see, then, how important it is to learn the correct words before going to school. Wouldn't it be terrible to have to go to the bathroom and not know the right word to ask the teacher so you can be excused?

When I was a little boy in the first grade I was too embarrassed to tell the teacher I had to be excused because I didn't know the right word to use. I asked her if I could leave the room to get a drink of water. She told me no. So I had to sit at my desk until I wet my pants. I was terribly embarrassed. Later the teacher told me I could have asked her to be excused. I now know that there was nothing to be embarrassed about, but I wish I had known the right words. Some still won't use those words and prefer just to say that they need to go to the toilet. This is okay too.

There are many ways of having fun with language. Little children like to invent words. Perhaps you like to make rhymes, or riddles—or you may think it is fun to learn new, hard words and try them out on your friends. Why not learn a new word now and try it out on your friends? The word is *epidermis* (ep-i-DER-mis) and it means the outer layer of skin. Maybe tomorrow you can say to one of your friends, "My epidermis itches," and see what he says.

Many boys and girls seem to think that it is amusing or "smart" to use vulgar language when they talk about their bodies—especially when they talk about members of the opposite sex. Possibly these boys and girls just don't know the right words because they've never been taught. Or maybe they think that since some ignorant grown-ups use vulgar words or they have heard them on TV that it makes them seem grown-up too if they use them. They don't know that it also makes them seem ignorant.

Have you ever used such language trying to impress someone? Did you know that Jesus said, "And I tell you this, that you must give account on judgment day for every idle word you speak" (Matthew 12:36, *Living Gospels*)? Jesus also said, "A good man's speech reveals the rich treasures within him. An evil-hearted man is filled with venom, and his speech reveals it" (Matthew 12:35, *Living Gospels*).

It is part of growing up to learn how to speak correctly of one's body and not to joke too much about it or to make embarrassing jokes about someone else's body. Remember—your body is the temple of the Holy Spirit. So make it a practice to learn, and to use, the right words about your body—and about sex.

Feelings Grow Up Too

When you were a baby you cried easily when you were hurt, hungry or uncomfortable. Crying was the only way of calling someone to help you, for you could do very little to help yourself. By now, however, you have learned many ways of getting yourself out of trouble without crying for help. You see, your feelings grow up, too.

Patience is one of the things you learn as you grow up. When you were a little baby you had little patience. If you wanted your bottle, or a toy, or your diaper changed—you wanted it right away, that very minute. As you grow older, though, you often plan ahead for something you want and you learn that sometimes you have to wait to get the things you want.

LET'S TALK ABOUT LIFE

Your feelings toward your parents change too. When you were a little baby you loved them simply because they were there to take care of you. In fact, you would have probably loved anyone else just as much as your real parents if they'd been there to take care of you and shower their love on you. Remember, I said my baby sister was adopted. She never knew her real parents, because her mother was not able to take care of her and raise her as a daughter. This mother still loved her daughter, but the best way she could show her love was to let someone else (in this case, my parents) take the little girl and raise her as their own daughter. This little baby didn't know. She was too small to understand. All she cared about was having someone to love her and take care of her. As she grew older she learned to love my parents as if they were her real parents, for this is the way love is.

As you grow older your love for your parents becomes more mature. When you were two or three years old you loved your parents mostly because they loved you. Now that you are older you may love them more for what they are—and for who they are.

You probably also show your love differently. As a little child you used to hug their necks and kiss them. Now you like to think ahead, and plan to buy them presents, or help your mother in the kitchen, or help your dad in the yard. One third-grade boy I know shows his love by getting up early each morning and emptying all the trash baskets in the house into the garbage can before he goes to school. This is a nice way to show love, because love can be spelled in another way—H-E-L-P!

When you were a small baby, you needed to be near

Growing and Learning

your mother most of the time. Even when you started to kindergarten or first grade you may have felt unhappy about being left in a strange place without her. Now that you have been in school for several years, you don't mind being away from home most of the morning and afternoon. You have made new friends, and you may ride your bicycle to visit them, even though they live a long way from you. It may be that you belong to some groups like the Cub Scouts or church groups, or maybe you are playing ball on a school or recreation league team. If this is so, it means you are spending more time away from your home than you did when you were a baby. But this does not mean you love your family less. It just means you are growing up, and your feelings are growing up at the same time. You are gradually becoming more independent as you grow.

Your feelings about your body also change as you grow up. For example, little babies do not think anything about modesty or immodesty. Sometimes little babies, even after they learn how to walk, will run through the house without any clothes on. They don't care who sees them naked. As boys and girls grow older, however, they learn to develop a sense of privacy about their bodies.

Do you remember the passage of Scripture we looked at a few pages back when Paul said, "Yes, we are especially glad to have some parts [of the body] that seem rather odd! And we carefully protect from the eyes of others those parts that should not be seen" (1 Corinthians 12:23, *Living Letters*). When you were a little baby you didn't think about this at all, but now that you're growing up, you think about it more often. Maybe your mother or father made some snapshots of you when you

LET'S TALK ABOUT LIFE

were a tiny baby—and you were naked. Does it embarrass you now if they show these snapshots to their friends? You see, God has let grow in you the desire to wear clothes and to develop a sense of privacy about your body.

As you know, it is the custom to wear different kinds of clothes in different places. The clothes you wear for swimming are not the kind you wear to school. Probably in school, after your physical education classes, you will be showering or changing clothes in the presence of others of your own sex.

Boys will notice that some boys have been *circumcised* (ser-kum-SIZED) while others have not. This means that soon after the boy baby is born the doctor cuts away some of the loose skin overlying the end of the penis. Many parents, but not all, have their boy babies circumcised. If you have not been circumcised you need to take special care in washing your penis to be sure it is clean.

Your body is nothing to be ashamed of or embarrassed about, because God made your body, and the Bible says that God looked upon all that He had made and said, "It is good." It was only after Adam and Eve sinned that they grew ashamed of their nakedness. God does not want us to be ashamed of our bodies, but He does want us to dress modestly. In some homes, members of the family prefer to dress and undress privately. In other homes members of the family may undress in front of other family members. In some homes, it is a custom to close the bathroom door when it is in use; in other homes, the bathroom door is never closed. In all homes, however, some form of modesty is taught.

There are many different customs about modesty and

Growing and Learning

about keeping one's body covered. These differences are not really very important. It is not surprising that boys and girls in one family, or one school, or one section of the country may have different feelings about these things. You yourself will probably change some of your own ideas as you grow older.

Some of your friends may have some peculiar ideas about the bodies of the opposite sex. This is because they have never been taught the facts. To be sure that your own ideas are correct, you may want to read this book again and talk about it with your mother and father, your minister, a youth worker at the church, or a teacher. Some other good books you might like to read are listed on page 111.

Even Friendships Change as You Grow

As you grow older, your feelings toward members of the same sex and toward members of the opposite sex will change. Little babies don't care whether their playmates are boy babies or girl babies. Even in nursery school and kindergarten little children play together without caring whether their playmates are boys or girls.

But by now, if you're a girl, you probably don't enjoy playing with boys. You have more fun when you're with your girlfriends. If you're a boy you probably have some very strong feelings against playing with girls. You'd rather have your own gang of boys, or play with some pal. That's fine. There's nothing wrong with that. But don't be surprised, if, after a few years, things begin to change. Maybe they're already changing. Maybe some of your friends like to have a special boy or a special girl as a good friend. That's all right too. Remember, no boy is just like another boy, nor is any girl just like another girl. However, after a while, you'll

LET'S TALK ABOUT LIFE

probably start feeling good when a member of the opposite sex pays some attention to you. You'll probably blush and feel funny when someone kids you about having a boyfriend or a girlfriend. As you keep growing, you'll soon find that if you're a girl, boys are pretty interesting after all. And if you're a boy, you'll find out that girls aren't so bad either.

FILL IN THE BLANK

1. List some ways you can show your mother how you love her by helping _____.

2. List some ways you can show your father how much you love him by helping _____.

3. List three of your special friends. _____, _____, _____.

4. How old were you when you stopped wearing a diaper? _____.

5. If you are a boy, have you been circumcised? Yes____ No____.

CHAPTER EIGHT
Looking Forward to Changes

Looking Forward to Changes

How your body will change

How girls change

How boys change

Growing up may seem awfully far away, but it won't be long before you're in junior high. Then comes senior high school, and after that, college or maybe the military service, a job, getting married, making your own home and having children. Before you know it, you'll be a grandmother or grandfather shaking your head about "the younger generation...."

Before you grow up, however, you will go through several years when some big changes take place in your body. These changes will affect your feelings, the things you enjoy doing, even your ability to make decisions. This period of several years is called *adolescence* (ad-uh-LES-ens), and the first part of this period is called *puberty* (PYOO-ber-tee), which is the time that your physical body grows up. If you are a girl, your body begins to make mature egg cells. If you are a boy, your body begins to make mature sperm cells. People usually

LET'S TALK ABOUT LIFE

call the teenage years, adolescent years.

You will also notice some annoying outward changes in your body. Your face may seem "oily," and you will have pimples on your cheeks, chin, neck and back. There will also be a change in your "sweat," so that your body may have an unpleasant odor when you perspire. Because of this, you will need to take a daily soap bath, gently scrubbing your face, neck and shoulders. Use of an underarm deodorant will make it more pleasing for others to be around you.

If you have brothers and sisters in their teens, you know that teenagers sometimes feel themselves to be more grown-up than their parents think they are. Perhaps both are right! Teenagers are often more grown than their parents want to admit but are not actually as grown as they think they are. But adolescence is a very interesting time, for it is a time of growing, trying new things, studying and learning. It is also a time of high ideals, lofty dreams and ambitions, and, sometimes, great disappointments. It is one of the greatest times of life and something you should look forward to with much anticipation.

How Your Body Will Change

Do you remember, in the first chapter of this book, that we talked about a spurt of fast growth in height that happens to most girls when they are 10 or 12 and to most boys when they are 12 or 14? Before this spurt of growing is over, several parts of your body will begin to change. The first change is inward and you won't notice it. Inside your body are several small organs called *glands*. These glands make certain kinds of chemicals called *hormones* (HOR-mones). When God signals a "time to grow up" these glands send the hormones into

Looking Forward to Changes

the blood.

The master gland is the *pituitary* (pih-TYOO-uh-ter-ee) gland. It is about as big as a large green pea or small marble and is located underneath your brain, deep inside your skull. It is hard to believe that such a tiny part of your body can be as important as this part is. This gland makes several different hormones. One of them regulates your height and size by controlling the way your bones grow. You may have seen pictures of giants and dwarfs. Probably the giants had more of this hormone and the dwarfs less. However, nearly all children have just enough for them to grow up to a normal height.

This gland also makes your sex glands mature at a certain age. The sex glands are the ovaries and the testicles. The ovaries make the female egg cells and the testicles make a male sperm cells. These glands (the sex glands) produce the hormones that make girls look like women and boys look like men.

As the brain sends signals to these glands they begin to send their hormones into the bloodstream to circulate all over the body—and the first signs of adolescence then appear. This is God's way of telling your body that it is time to stop being a child—and time to start growing up. The writer of Ecclesiastes said, "Remember now thy Creator in the days of thy youth..." (Ecclesiastes 12:1). What better time to remember the wonderful way God has made you than when you feel that first surge of growing up in your body and glance in the mirror and see that you are really beginning to grow up.

How Girls Change

Remember we said that when a baby girl is born, her ovaries and egg cells are not fully grown? When girls are about 11 or 12, the hormone of the pituitary gland that affects these glands causes changes to take place in the body.

Then what happens? She is likely to grow taller and slimmer, although she is gaining weight. Her hips broaden and round out, and her breasts grow larger. The hormones also cause hair to grow under her arms and in a little triangle across the lower part of the abdomen in what is known as the pubic region. The girl's voice becomes richer and fuller.

A girl is sometimes troubled if she develops more rapidly than other girls of her age. One girl may have well-developed breasts at the age of 11 while all the girls in her class are still flat-chested. But in just a short time the other girls will start developing too, and soon all of them will look like teenage girls.

This new growth makes her attractive, and it is useful too, for God is preparing the young lady for motherhood. The widening of the hips gives her body a form more suitable for having a baby some day. The breasts develop so she can nurse a child when the time comes.

All these things may take several years for completion. Then, when the girl is about 13 (although it sometimes happens earlier and sometimes later) her ovaries begin to make fully grown egg cells. After that, an egg cell leaves an ovary about once a month.

Every time an egg cell leaves an ovary, the lining of the uterus fills with an extra supply of blood as the uterus gets ready to take care of a fertilized egg. If the egg is not fertilized, that is, if there is no male sperm cell to form a baby, it leaves the body painlessly a week or so later through the vagina. This will be accompanied by some blood and the inner lining of the uterus. This is called *menstruation* (men-stroo-ay-shun). Menstrua-

Looking Forward to Changes

tion begins about 10 to 14 days after the egg leaves the ovary and about seven to 10 days after the unfertilized egg disappears.

You remember that if an egg cell is fertilized (if it comes in contact with a male sperm cell), it attaches itself to the lining of the uterus and stays there while it grows into a baby. In this case the extra blood is needed, and it does not leave the body. One of the signs that a baby has started to grow is that menstruation does not occur.

It is a very proud and happy day in the life of a girl when she notices the first slight discharge of blood from her vagina. It is nothing to fear. Rather, it is something for which to thank God and rejoice—for it is on this day that she has evidence that she has indeed become a young woman and will be able to have her own children later on.

Menstruation usually occurs for the first time after the other changes in the girl's body have begun. After menstruation has started, a girl may expect it to occur about once a month until she is middle-aged—usually sometime in her 40s or 50s. However, young girls who have just begun to menstruate may frequently have a month or several months when they do not menstruate.

Menstruation usually lasts just a few days each month. Some girls have mild abdominal cramps or aching in the lower back, particularly on the first day. It is a normal process, and most girls feel entirely well during the menstrual period. It is not a sickness, and as a rule, girls can continue their normal activity in every way. Personal cleanliness, though, is very important. Warm soapy showers or sponge bathing of the pubic area at least once a day should be part of a girl's regular routine.

LET'S TALK ABOUT LIFE

To protect clothing during menstruation, girls wear sanitary pads or napkins. A small elastic belt is sometimes used to hold the pad in place or the pad must just fit in her panties. It can be changed as often as needed. Some girls prefer to use a tampon. This is a tight little roll of absorbent material which is inserted into the vagina. It absorbs the waste blood, and can be withdrawn and thrown away. Before using tampons, a girl should talk with her family doctor to be sure there is no reason not to use them.

After menstruation is over, the ovaries are ready to release another fully grown egg cell that will start on the same journey all over again.

Some girls speak of menstruation as their "period," because it usually comes periodically, about every 28 days at a regular time. All this is part of God's design for the continuation of life. Without it, no woman could ever have a baby.

How Boys Change

The same pituitary gland that sends hormones into the girl's bloodstream and causes the changes in her body also brings about changes in boys. When boys are 12 or so, they have an increased amount of hormones. Soon afterward, the testicles begin to make hormones that cause the boy's body to change. Immediately you begin to notice a difference in your body.

Perhaps the first change you notice will be in your voice. Boys usually have high voices until their bodies begin to change; then their voices lower and deepen. Hair begins to grow on the lower part of the boy's abdomen around his penis. Later it grows under his arms. About this same time boys begin to get hair on their chests. Soon the boy will be looking into the mirror and

Looking Forward to Changes

feeling his chin, wondering when it will be time to begin shaving.

While all this is going on, the body takes on a different look. The penis and testicles grow larger, and the boy's shoulders begin to broaden. He begins to take on the look of a man, although inside he may still feel very much like a boy. He begins to try to act "grown-up."

During these teenage years, it may happen that a boy's penis becomes stiff and erect. This can be caused by several things. Sometimes at night, if the bladder fills with urine, the pressure from having to go to the bathroom will cause an erection. If this is the case, then simply going to the bathroom to urinate will allow it to return to its normal size. At other times, however, the penis may become erect during the night, and semen is discharged unexpectedly. This is called a *seminal emission* (sem-i-nal e-mish-un). It is a natural thing to happen, just as the changes that take place in the body are natural. It is not "sinful" or to be feared. It is God's way of allowing the boy to discharge semen when the pressure builds up inside the testicles. It may be accompanied by a dream, and thus is called a "wet dream" since the fluid may wet your pajamas as you sleep.

Sometimes boys and girls become curious about their own sex organs and occasionally will play with or fondle them. We need to remember that our bodies are the temple of the Holy Spirit, and we should conduct ourselves properly at all times—not ever doing in private what we would be ashamed for others to know about. The sex organs, like all other parts of our body, are created by God. However, we should not exhibit these "private" parts of our body, but should maintain modesty in dress and action.

LET'S TALK ABOUT LIFE

After the sex organs have matured, and growth in height has slowed down or stopped, young people still have some growing up to do before they are ready to be fully "on their own." There are many things to learn about how to earn a living, how to make a home and how to take care of themselves before they are ready to marry and have children of their own. The years in junior high and senior high school are good years for learning some of these things.

In high school, boys and girls make many new friends and have a lot of fun working and playing together. Having many friends will help you learn something about how to choose a husband or a wife. Right now, at your age, your father and mother are your best helpers in choosing your friends. Your church is a good place to have your first contact and your home is the best place to bring your friends for a good time. There is nothing better than a happy family living in a happy home.

Growing up physically and sexually is important, but it is only part of the process of becoming an adult. Jesus grew four ways. He "increased in wisdom and stature and in favor with God and man" (Luke 2:52). In other words, He developed intellectually, physically, spiritually and socially. Jesus should be your ideal to follow. Remember He was once the same age you are now— and the same changes you are going through, He went through also.

But even more important, remember He is still alive today. Jesus is living in this world today in the presence of the Holy Spirit. In fact, it is the Holy Spirit who gives us the power to overcome temptation, to live pure lives, and to glorify God's Son, Jesus.

Jesus knows the problems you face. He will stay

Looking Forward to Changes

beside you all the time. He is the finest friend and companion you can ever have.

FILL IN THE BLANK

1. List three changes to expect in a girl's body when she enters puberty:_____
_____
_____.

2. List three changes to expect in a boy's body when he enters puberty:_____
_____
_____.

3. Where is your pituitary gland located? _____.

WORDS YOU SHOULD KNOW

Abdomen (AB-duh-men) The lower part of the midsection of the belly.

Adolescence (ad-uh-LES-ens) The time of life between childhood and adulthood; the teen years.

Circumcision (ser-kum-SIZH-un) A minor operation, usually performed soon after the birth of a boy baby, in which the loose skin (foreskin) is removed from the end of the penis.

Conception (kon-SEP-shun) The joining of the male sperm cell with the female egg cell to start a new life.

Fallopian tube (fal-O-pee-un) The tubes that lead from the ovaries to the uterus in the abdomen of the female. These tubes hold the egg until it is time to let the unfertilized cell leave the body.

LET'S TALK ABOUT LIFE

Fertilize (FER-ti-lyze) To make fertile by the union of the male sperm cell with the female egg cell; to make pregnant.

Fetus (FEE-tus) The unborn baby after eight weeks or more of growth in the mother's uterus.

Gland (GLAND) An organ that forms one or more substances to be used in, or eliminated from, the body.

Heredity (hehr-ED-i-tee) The characteristics passed on from parents to children.

Hormone (HOR-mone) A substance produced by a gland and carried into the bloodstream to stimulate other parts of the body.

Labor (LAY-bor) The pains of childbirth as the mother's body pushes to give birth to her baby.

Menstruation (men-stroo-AY-shun) The monthly flow of waste blood and tissue from the uterus.

Navel (NAY-vel) The depression in the middle of the abdomen at the point where the umbilical cord was attached while the baby was in the mother's uterus (your "belly-button").

Ovary (OH-vuh-ree) One of the two organs in the female abdomen that produces the egg cells.

Penis (PEE-nis) The male sex organ through which both urine and semen pass out of the body.

Words You Should Know

Pituitary (pih-TYOO-uh-ter-ee) The body's master gland located deep inside the skull. Its secretions control and regulate many other organs.

Placenta (pla-SEN-tuh) A special network of blood vessels and tissues that develop on the lining of the uterus during pregnancy, to which the umbilical cord runs from the growing child in which food, oxygen, and wastes are exchanged between mother and child.

Pregnant (PREG-nant) Carrying a growing baby in the uterus.

Premature (pree-ma-TYOOR) Too early. Coming before the proper time, as a baby being born before the usual nine months of pregnancy have passed.

Puberty (PYOO-ber-tee) The time of becoming mature when the sex organs begin to develop.

Scrotum (SKROH-tum) The external sac of skin in which the testicles hang between the legs of a male.

Semen (SEE-men) The male fertilizing fluid, composed of sperm and the whitish fluid in which they are suspended.

Seminal emission (SEM-i-nal em-MISH-un) The discharge of semen from the penis.

Sexual intercourse (sex-U-al IN-ter-course) The act of discharging male sperm cells from the father's penis into the mother's vagina.

Sonogram (SAWN-uh-gram) An X-ray-like picture of a baby inside the mother's body made with sound waves.

Sperm (SPERM) The male cell produced in the testicles.

Testicle (TESS-ti-kal) One of the two male reproductive glands which produce sperm. They are contained in the scrotum and are the shape of a small pecan.

Umbilical (um-BIL-i-kal) The cord of the circulatory system running from the unborn baby's abdomen to the mother's placenta, through which the fetus is provided with food and oxygen and through which waste is carried away.

Uterus (YOO-ter-us) The hollow female organ for housing and feeding a baby during its development before birth.

Vagina (va-JY-nuh) The passage leading from the uterus to the outside of the body, between a girl's legs.

Virgin (VER-jin) A person who has never had sexual intercourse.

SOME OTHER HELPFUL BOOKS

Hummel, Ruth Stevenson. *Wonderfully Made*. Concordia Publishing House, St. Louis, London, 1967. One of a series of six, published by the Lutheran Church Missouri Synod for grades four and six. Beautifully illustrated and written from a sound Christian perspective.

Scheinfeld, Amran. *Why You Are You*. London, New York, Abelard-Schuman, 1968. The author combines psychological, sociological, and anthropological insights to give children a well-rounded understanding of themselves and other people.

Taylor, Kenneth N. *Almost Twelve*. Tyndale House, Wheaton, Illinois, 1968. The translator of *Living Letters* and *The Living New Testament* tells the simple story of human reproduction as the author has told it to his own children. Written from a beautiful Christian viewpoint.

Whiting, Ellis W. *The Story of Life*. Story of Life Publishing Company, Appleton, Wisconsin, 1933. A schoolteacher writes to his little 6-year-old daughter about "Where do babies come from?" A bit elementary for fifth and sixth graders but very fundamental and sound.